HIDDEN TREASURES

WESTERN SURREY

Edited by Natalie Nightingale

First published in Great Britain in 2002 by
YOUNG WRITERS
Remus House,
Coltsfoot Drive,
Peterborough, PE2 9JX
Telephone (01733) 890066

HB ISBN 0 75432 865 1
SB ISBN 0 75432 866 X

FOREWORD

This year, the Young Writers' Hidden Treasures competition proudly presents a showcase of the best poetic talent from over 72,000 up-and-coming writers nationwide.

Young Writers was established in 1991 and we are still successful, even in today's technologically-led world, in promoting and encouraging the reading and writing of poetry.

The thought, effort, imagination and hard work put into each poem impressed us all, and once again, the task of selecting poems was a difficult one, but nevertheless, an enjoyable experience.

We hope you are as pleased as we are with the final selection and that you and your family continue to be entertained with *Hidden Treasures Western Surrey* for many years to come.

CONTENTS

Mytchett Primary School

Scott Hagan	1
Hayley Evans	2
Kerri Simmonds	3
Chloe Deakin	4
Katie Lemon	5
Victoria Filshie	6
Daly George	7
Corrinne Ann Padwick	8
Gary Holford	9
Natalie Watkinson	10
Austin Surey	11
Suzy Fenge	12
Alice Surey	13
Ryan Lee-Manning	14
Sam Bennett	15

Potters Gate School

Greg Kane	16
Pauline Nottingham	17
Patience Nottingham	18
Libby Runham	19
Rhea Sinclair	20
Claudia Turkington	21
Sebastian Foster-Postnikov	22
Oliver Rooney	23
Amy McGuigan	24
Jason Sampson	25
Evie Leedale	26
Amy Bills	27
Bo Franklin	28
Madeleine Cumming	29
Jessica Kane	30
Josephine Morris	31
William Corry	32

St Augustine's Primary School, Camberley

Louise McGovern	33
Daniel Barclay	34
Ryan Tate	35
Michelle Quinn	36
George Simpson	37
Shaun Miles	38
Laura Boyle	39
Sam Cunningham	40
Suzanna Withers	41
Michael Everard	42
Jake Cahill	43
Jack Farnon	44
Abbie Moran	45
Nick Lardner	46
Rachel Banks	47
George Pilling	48
John Mageean	49
Natalie Garland	50
Claire Gallagher	51
Alex Lowe	52
Joe Holt	53
Thomas Saunders	54
Hannah Patel	55

St Catherine's School, Camberley

Georgia Oakes	56
Serena Burton	57
Abbey Perria	58
Jennifer Abel	59
Victoria Beynon	60
Rachael Curtin	61
Roseanna Leney	62
Sarah Lapthorn	63
Grace Farrell	64
Kesleigh Withers	65
Claire Jones	66
Sable Fitzgerald	67

Emma Blott	68
Elizabeth Anders	69
Hannah Martin	70
Melanie Lovell	71
Imogen Tillman	72
Emma Kendall	73
Farrah Amin	74
Esme Langford	75
Hannah Church	76
Caitlin Parker	77
Niccita Singh	78
Tedi Basham	79
Anna Bagramova	80
Colleen Perria	81

St Peter's CE (Aided) Primary School, Farnham

Hollie Southey	82
Sophie Paine	83
Zachary Wynne	84
Josh Loftus	85
Mason Redman	86
Ella Bennett	87
Andrew Jackson	88
Thomas Graham	89
Chloe Goode	90
Rebecca Cooles	91
Adam Marchment	92
Lesley Green	93
Matthew Brown	94
Josh Injai	95
Jacqueline Nevill	96
Matthew Bolton	97
Emma Marriott	98
Charlotte Bryant	99

The Poems

THE WET AND THE DRY

The rainforest is pouring with rain
Like snow coming down on a winter's day
The ground has been flooded by the water's flow
No one could get past it because it will cover you from head to toe
The desert is scorching like lava from a volcano
The camel walks past the boiling sun
Like an ant walking across a radiator
The fish stays in one place under the sun in a fish tank.

Scott Hagan (11)
Mytchett Primary School

ME!

Happy and smiling all the time
About and everywhere
Yellow is the sun, yellow is my hair
Loving and caring
Energetic and fast
Yeap, that's me *Hayley.*

Hayley Evans (11)
Mytchett Primary School

ANIMALS ALPHABET

A is for thousands of little ants
C is for the cat purring all day
E is for the enormous elephant
G is for the long necked giraffe
I   is for iguana that crawls around
K is for the jumping kangaroo
M is for the swinging monkey
O is for the octopus with eight legs
R is for the great rhino
T is for the stripy tiger
V is for the raging vulture flying through the sky
Z is for the black and white zebra.

Kerri Simmonds (11)
Mytchett Primary School

THE WET AND THE DRY BY THE SEA

Drenched creatures in the sea,
Like water in a bath.
Shells, stones and seaweed
All that cannot see us,
But dry on the outside
And soaking within.
Children swimming and shrieking loudly
Like fish swimming and lions roaring.
Drenched creatures sleeping calmly
Like statues underwater,
Not swimming in their sleep,
All except the shark.
But the people on the sand don't care about them
Like lonely children on the street.
People making sandcastles
Like builders making houses.
   Children paddling
      Not leaving
         Getting soaked
            The sun shines
All go home
   Nice and dry
      Go to bed.

Chloe Deakin (10)
Mytchett Primary School

DOWN IN THE JUNGLE

Down in the jungle
Down deep in the jungle
Where nobody goes
There was a rhino
The rhino was having a bath
He was having a bath in mud
Down deeper in the jungle
There was a parrot
The parrot was on a branch
He was on a branch nesting
Further north of the jungle
There was a monkey
The monkey was up a tree
He was up a tree swinging from branch to branch
South east of the jungle
There was a snake
The snake was on the ground
He was slithering around looking for prey.

Katie Lemon (10)
Mytchett Primary School

MY NAME (HAIKU)

V   It flies out for food,
    The vulture swoops for the kill,
    The vulture flies home.

I   They are very small,
    Insects are all around us,
    Even in your home.

C   Cats are domestic,
    But some live in the wild,
    They are night creepers.

T   Lays eggs on the beach,
    The turtle swims all day long,
    On a summer's day.

O   An otter is small,
    Living in the cold rivers,
    Swimming to its home.

R   The rat looked around,
    The rat is a small rodent
    Living in cages.

I   Iris is pretty,
    Comes out in early summer,
    It has spiky leaves.

A   Ants live in ant hills,
    They help each other find food,
    Stumbling over cracks.

Victoria Filshie (10)
Mytchett Primary School

STILL AND MOVING

Still in a rainforest trees are taking years to get sunlight on their leaves
Birds laying their nest ready for their babies to come
Creatures on the ground are rustling around
Flying squirrels jumping from tree to tree
Frogs are leaping onto lilypads.

Snails are still because they are in their shells
Plants are growing slowly that's why they are still
Branches and trees join together to get higher and higher
Bees flying into beehives
Squirrels jumping from tree to tree like they are trying to fly
Vines killing trees by strangling them
Bats on branches sleeping.

Daly George (10)
Mytchett Primary School

PEACE AND NOISE UNDERWATER

The peaceful water bubbling
Under the surface of the sea
Like a child blowing down a straw
All is silent by the floating coral
Where coloured fishes sleep
Like frozen people acting like a stone
The noise of worried fish
As the shark searches for prey
Like a starved lion and his pride
The sound of fish scurrying away
Away from the creature of the deep
Like leaves on a windy morning.

The dawn finally awakens
All is quiet under the salty sea
Like a mouse tiptoeing into its hole
Everything is calm and peaceful
Under the blending horizon
Like trees gently swaying
Suddenly the irritating diver jumps into the sleepy land
Like a kangaroo in a zoo
All of the fish scatter away
In and out of the rocky holes
Like a stampede of elephants
The diver returns to the floating boat
All is quiet and calm.

Corrinne Ann Padwick (10)
Mytchett Primary School

SUNSETS

Sunsets echo in the distance
Animals cheeping amongst the leaves
Darker and darker waving trees
Sun rises again and again
Leaves whooshing down the stream
Jumping fish again and again
Sun shining through the trees, morning is here again.

Echoes coming from the birds
Trees wobbling from the wind, heavier and heavier
Leaves falling amongst this everywhere
Branches snapping off the trees
Sunsets lower and lower
It's night again.

Gary Holford (10)
Mytchett Primary School

NAME HAIKU

N   The nightingale flies
    Soaring through the windy air
    Singing so sweetly.

A   Ants, small and tiny
    Marching back to their ant hill
    Carrying some food.

T   Plodding slowly home
    Upon a hot summer's day
    Tortoise will get there.

A   Alligator's snap
    Cooling down in the river
    Waiting for his food.

L   Lion - full of pride
    Roaring and shaking his mane
    While eyeing its prey.

I   Iguana, green
    Lazily lying around
    In the baking sun.

E   Elephants are huge
    Sucking water up their trunks
    Making lots of noise.

Natalie Watkinson (11)
Mytchett Primary School

WINTER'S NIGHT

While cringing across the motionless floor,
a fox is hunting.
His paws are like ice,
his face is melancholy.
This way or that, this way or that?
'Where is my prey?' he speculates.
Trees glistening in the silvery sky,
so radiant, it could blind a wise rat.
The fox still fawns, covering his eyes
when in the moonlight,
and quaking when placing a foot in the
frigid streams.
Soon he begins to change to whether
he will survive this,
    winter's night!

Austin Surey (11)
Mytchett Primary School

WELSH MORNING

Buzzards hover over a field,
Circling closer, closer, closer.
Wings fold back, neck unveiled,
Down like a bomb, a bullet, a dagger.

A fox creeps through a meadow,
Sniffing the morning breeze,
A cockerel makes a last show,
Of his colourful tail to the hens.

A barn owl flies over the hill,
Extending his talons he swoops,
As a duck washes its bill,
In the early morning flood.

The blood of a hare waters the leaves,
The feathers of a cockerel
Spread about the courtyard
And the cry of a dying weasel.

Like the victimised creatures,
The blood of light runs into the valley as the sun doth rise.
And as the sun did rise o'er a hospital,
Inside an aunt did not awake,
Her life, like others, has ended of a cruel fate.

Suzy Fenge (11)
Mytchett Primary School

DESERT LIFE

The sun shone hot on the sand,
A light in the morning wake,
The stillness makes it seem unreal,
Like a photo or a painting.
Then, over the hot desert horizon,
An animal appears,
Like a ghost it glided t'wards the sun.
A vulture or a rat
Moving like a squirming worm across the golden sheen.

The sky is blue and clear,
With nothing in its way,
Like a sheet of clean blue canvas,
Hanging onto the easel of life.
The camels trudge through the golden land,
Like a tree endlessly growing.
The buzzing flies give life to the sky,
Like dormice to a cornfield.
Pushing up through the sand, a lizard
Like a flickering flame through the coal.

The sand is still, the sun is hot,
Birds fly and swoop.
This is a place where no one goes,
Where death seems unreal.

Alice Surey (11)
Mytchett Primary School

WINTER SNOW

Winter snow, crispy white
Falls gently day and night
More and more the day and night
Covering the earth snowy-white
Snow falls from the sky
Scattering over you and I
Frozen water covers lakes
Like a white silver skate.

Ryan Lee-Manning (10)
Mytchett Primary School

ANIMALS (HAIKU)

A Adders have poison
    On their backs they have zigzags
    Adders are deadly

N Nightingales sing well
    It's like an opera singer
    Singing gets higher

I   guanas' scales
    Green and very smooth to touch
    They are quite agile

M Monkeys have long tails
    They help them to climb up trees
    They are like humans

A Ants are very small
    And they have large colonies
    Working all the time

L Leopards are spotted
    Leopards sometimes live in trees
    They are carnivores.

Sam Bennett (10)
Mytchett Primary School

THE TRAVELLER'S TALE

Long ago when war was common,
everybody was greatly solemn.
But there was a man who was not scared,
not frightened, anywhere.
And he had gone on a quest to see
how dangerous it was said to be,
even by his family.
And then one night when the stars were bright,
hanging up there in the air, he travelled east watching out for beasts
while heading for his family home.
For he had given his word that he would return somehow,
some day, and then when he saw the dark old door, he smiled.
He gave a sigh as he heard the song of the bluebird
drift beautifully away on its wings.
Then he stood there thinking as his feelings were sinking
from his broken heart to the floor.
(Why must it be no more?)

Greg Kane (10)
Potters Gate School

THE MAGIC BOX

I will put in the box
the flowering vine of Juliet
a string from the lyre of Apollo
the sprinkle of dust from a fairy's wing.

I will put in the box
the same wine that maddened Hercules
the bolt of lightning held by Zeus
the glistening heart of heaven.

I will put in the box
the poisonous tooth of a hydra
a white horse with wings
the swish of the wind.

I will put in the box
the angel Gabriel's halo
the end of the Earth
the mask of the man of the moon.

My box is fashioned from
emeralds and rock
with some fluffy clouds inside
and the keyhole of Cinderella's room.

I will fly in my box
skimming the candyfloss clouds
and dive down into the sparkling Pacific.

Pauline Nottingham (9)
Potters Gate School

HAPPYLAND

In Happyland everybody huggles
Everybody smiles, everybody laughs
Nobody frowns, nobody struggles
Everybody dances, full of cheer . . .
Help! Get me out of here!

Patience Nottingham (9)
Potters Gate School

THE MAGIC BOX

I will put in the box
a brown, hard, hairy apple falling off a palm tree
a smooth green coconut, lonely on an apple tree
the growing, winding stem of a flower.

I will put in the box
the first bark of a dog
the horn off a furious rhinosaurus
a soft feather from a multicoloured, magnificent bird.

Libby Runham (8)
Potters Gate School

THE MAGIC BOX

I will put in the box
the scent of fresh, fragrant roses
waking me up on a summer's morning
the gentle sound of a baby dolphin
glittering in the moonlight
and an eyelash from a grizzly brown bear.

I will put in the box
the sprinkle of dust from a fairy
the forgiveness of God inside the sun
and the strings of a golden harp.

Rhea Sinclair (9)
Potters Gate School

THE MAGIC BOX

I will put in the box
The lost, clever memories of Atlantis
An Atlantic boat sailing in the wind
The lost, forgotten continent of Atlantis.

I will put in the box
A big blue whale
The lapping blue waves of the Pacific
And a dolphin, the colour of the seas.

Claudia Turkington (8)
Potters Gate School

THE MAGIC BOX

I will put in the box
A big bright UFO about to land
A huge sea with a battle ship steaming along
And a Chinese dragon in a parade.

I will put in the box
The taste buds of a black bee
A bunch of feathers from a green eagle
A sword which is too blunt to fight.

I will put in the box
The hidden secrets from under the ground
A palm tree about to shrink
The feel of ancient bark.

I will put in the box
A photo of my best friend on a purring cloud
A feather in the softest pillow in the world
And a fast pink and purple frog eating candles.

Sebastian Foster-Postnikov (7)
Potters Gate School

THE MAGIC BOX

    I will put in the box
a pink apple on a palm tree
a snowman with a rumbling tum
a clock ticking backwards.

    I will put in the box
a flint from a stiganopythacas
007's golden gun
the taste of a chocolate fly.

Oliver Rooney (8)
Potters Gate School

THE MAGIC BOX

I will put in the box
A sparkling blue sea with no rushing waves
A palm tree in the middle of England
An apple tree in the Sahara desert.

I will put in the box
Some Romans from long ago
The sound of baby seals hawking at the Sealife Centre
The feelings of a baby smiling at you.

Amy McGuigan (9)
Potters Gate School

THE MAGIC BOX

I will put in the box
The sweet smell of strawberries on a summer's day
A yellow apple falling off a palm tree
The top of a volcano exploding with lava.

I will put in the box
A black and yellow bird with a shiny tail
An enormous tree blazing with fire
A tiny ant feeling his way through giant leaves.

I will put in the box
The voices of people laughing
The sound of an eagle catching his prey
The smell of a hippopotamus getting ready to charge.

Jason Sampson (8)
Potters Gate School

THE MAGIC BOX

I will put in the box
The blue feather of an eagle
The faint song of a robin
And the harsh, cold wind from the east.

I will put in the box
The flowering of the daffodil
The rushing wheels of a rollerblade
And the sweet cling of a coin.

Evie Leedale (8)
Potters Gate School

THE MAGIC BOX

I will put in the box . . .
African patterns on a gold whale,
The most colourful plant from a tropical rainforest,
A rainbow of a thousand colours in a shimmering dawn.
The lightning bolt from Zeus.

I will put in the box . . .
The glistening heart of heaven,
The smell of a precious geode from South America,
A palace made out of sparkling crystals.

I will put in the box . . .
An ancient underwater city made of gold,
The echoey sound of dolphins calling my name,
A wonderful feather from a purple peacock.

My box is embroidered with silk,
And dust from an angel's wing,
Inside there are beautiful petals from Asian flowers
And sequins on the bottom of the multicoloured box.

Amy Bills (9)
Potters Gate School

THE MAGIC BOX

I will put in the box
A house with four thousand windows
The moaning of a winter's night
A pink king in a green castle.

I will put in my box
Hercules fighting the hydra
The clicking of the keys on a keyboard
The laughing of a happy baby.

I will put in my box
The crying of multicoloured seagulls
The squeaking of a depressed hamster
The roaring of tigers in cages.

I will put in my box
The scent of an ancient rose
The black stripes of a tiger shark
The sound of a whale a mile away.

Bo Franklin (8)
Potters Gate School

THE MAGIC BOX

I will put in the box
an apple as yellow as a banana
the sounds of a dog barking
the sound of a whale wailing.

I will put in the box
an extra two seasons
a tabby dog and a Dalmatian cat
the sound of bricks scraping together.

Madeleine Cumming (8)
Potters Gate School

THE MAGIC BOX

I will put in the box
The great huge jaws of a silver shark
The crying of a small killer whale
A tiny piece of silk from a baby's christening dress.

I will put in the box
The ball of a tap shoe tapping on a wooden floor
The golden hair off my china doll
The king's head from an old coin.

I will put in the box
The feel of a baby's chubby cheeks
The soft touch of a peacock's feather
The rough, dark rock from the Red Sea.

Jessica Kane (8)
Potters Gate School

THE MAGIC BOX

I will put in the box
A tip of a white volcano with lava pouring out
A hair from the end of a grey African elephant's tail
A harp from a singing angel.

I will put in the box
A wing from a blood-thirsty dragon
An arrow from an ancient man
And the scent of a fresh daisy.

I will put in the box
A leaf rippling in the wind
The sound of the first bird ever
An ancient box growing smaller and smaller.

Josephine Morris (9)
Potters Gate School

FROZEN FINGERTIPS

Frozen fingertips
On the way to school
More frozen than ice
And stuck together like a pack of mice.

Frozen fingertips
On the way to work
So cold and stiff
And it's making me sniff - achoo!

Frozen fingertips
On the way to the park
They feel like stalactites
Stuck to iced glass.

Frozen fingertips
On the way to town
I'm going to buy some gloves
So my fingers won't be ice cold.

Now my fingertips are warm.

William Corry (8)
Potters Gate School

MY FAMILY

My mummy is like a teddy, all soft and cuddly.
My daddy is like a razor, all sharp and prickly.
My brother is like an old dog, he tires out too easily.
I can tell you one thing that's the same about them,
All are my family *and* not yours!

My nanny is like a collie who never lets you down.
My granny is like a glass ornament, rare and fragile.
My grandad is like a kitten, playful and friendly.
I can tell you one thing that's the same about them all,
They're my family *and* not yours!

My hamster Tiptoe is like an owl who sleeps at day, prowls at night.
My fish Rainbow is like a star shooting through the water.
My poochi Holly is like a bird who likes to play and sing.
I can tell you one thing that's the same about them all,
They're my family *and* not yours!

Louise McGovern (10)
St Augustine's Primary School, Camberley

FOOTBALL

My favourite sport is football
It keeps me healthy and fit
I play for Camberley Town
And I enjoy every bit.

I play in my school team
With the boys in my year
We have won lots of games
I'm the best player of the year.

Daniel Barclay (9)
St Augustine's Primary School, Camberley

ANTHONY, YOU'RE A STAR

Anthony you are so special
More than you will ever know
Our love will follow you
Wherever you shall go.

You're up above
Your star shines bright
Up with the doves
Especially at night.

This weekend you would have been one
And the fun would just have begun
Walking, talking, dribbling
Smiling, laughing, giggling.

We miss you Anthony
We always will
You're in our hearts
'Top of the charts'.

We know you're safe
In the best place
Where there is faith
But take care just in case.

God bless
Sleep tight
Angels on your pillows
Love Ryan.

Ryan Tate (9)
St Augustine's Primary School, Camberley

OUR MICE

My sister has a little mouse
I have got one too
When they're in their little house
They have a lot to do.

My sister's mouse is Pickles
She's sound asleep all day
Crawling on my hand it tickles
When she wants to play.

Kari is my mouse's name
The wheel is her best toy
It seems to be her favourite game
She gives me lots of joy.

Feeding them is lots of fun
A treat's a small cheese bite
We give it when the cleaning's done
And we put them away for the night.

Michelle Quinn (9)
St Augustine's Primary School, Camberley

MY MUM

I really, really love my mum,
she cheers me up when I am glum.
She always helps me sort things out,
I know she loves me, there's no doubt!

Mum always has a smiling face,
she can wash up quicker than a horse in a race.
My mum is more special than the rest,
and would come first if she took a test.

My mum smells sweeter than a rose,
I follow her around wherever she goes.
Her smile is like the brightest sun,
she makes the whole world so much fun.

Her hands are very small and neat,
her hair's as gold as fields of wheat.
She always has a gentle touch,
I love my mum so very much!

George Simpson (10)
St Augustine's Primary School, Camberley

THE LIGHT AT THE END OF THE TUNNEL

My life is getting better
Every single day
Because that shining little light
Is sparkling through the day.

So when I lay awake at night
I shall not be afraid
I like that little light
Keeping monsters and things away.

Now I fall asleep all snuggled up in bed
I say goodbye to the light
Until we meet again!

Shaun Miles (9)
St Augustine's Primary School, Camberley

MY PETS

Tabby was a rabbit
She was black and white
Her fur was soft to touch
Her eyes shone so bright
She'd hop around all day
Never sleep at night.

Gordon was a guinea pig
His coat was white and hairy
His eyes were devil red
And sometimes he was scary!
But if you should approach too quick
He was jolly wary.

Tabby used to boss Gordon around
She liked to rule the hutch
They both liked to nip
So we couldn't pick them up much
Perhaps that was because Gordon was an albino and
Tabby was a Dutch!

Laura Boyle (9)
St Augustine's Primary School, Camberley

BLANKY

Blanky, oh Blanky, oh where have you been?
You hide so well you cannot be seen.

Blanky, oh Blanky, I looked high and low,
You went so quietly and I did not know.

When you were gone I felt so sad,
Your disappearance was too bad.

When I find you I shall be
As happy as a fish in the sea.

Whilst I'm looking I'll think of when
We shall be together again.

You weren't behind the toy box, you weren't under my bed,
Don't remember leaving you in the garden shed.

I've looked in every cranny, I've looked in every nook,
One thing is for certain, you'll be in the last place I look!

Sam Cunningham (10)
St Augustine's Primary School, Camberley

SEASONS

Sunny blue skies fill people's hearts with happiness
Umbrellas shade us from the hot sun rays
Mad mosquitoes bite in the early evening
Magnificent blooms of flowers burst in the early summer
Eager children lick ice creams by the beach
Red sunsets end the day like a glowing fire.

Autumn leaves are red and yellow
Uncles and aunts pack away their summer clothes
Trickling raindrops fall down the windows
Ugly clouds chase each other across the sky
Moles come out of their holes at night to search for food
Noisy children stamp in the fallen leaves.

Wild winter beckons nearer
Ice starts to cover lakes
Noisy children are eager to build snowmen
Toys for Christmas appear in shops
Excited children wait to perform their plays about Jesus
Reindeer and Santa begin to arrive.

Sheep give birth to little lambs
Pussy willow hangs like lamb tails
Rabbits hop around from place to place
In gardens flowers grow again
Nights are getting shorter, evenings are getting lighter
Gone is the snow
The grass is cut and fresh.

Suzanna Withers (10)
St Augustine's Primary School, Camberley

THE SPACE EXPLORER

My rocket blasts off into space
Ever higher my spirits race
Flying further from the sun
Outer space, here I come!

I see a planet, lonely and cold
Should I land? Am I that bold?
I name it Helix as I touch down
Upon the cold and icy ground

Icy mountains, drifts of snow
Is there life? I do not know
All too soon back home I fly
Away from the planet, cold and dry

Soon I'm down on the launching pad
Back on Earth, half glad, half sad.

Michael Everard (10)
St Augustine's Primary School, Camberley

HERBY MCFEE

Inside the house of number three,
there lived a hamster called Herby McFee.
He liked to roam about the house
and meet up with his friend called Mouse.
They looked like twins because they were both white,
their first meeting gave them quite a fright.
They loved their secret hiding place,
deep inside the family suitcase.
But one sunny day their secret was over,
Mum had won the lottery rollover.
Down came the case for the family vacation,
Herby and Mouse had to find a new location!

The good thing is they found a new place to hide,
behind the teapot, on the side.
The family returned from their summer holiday,
Herby and Mouse heard the dad say,
'Who would like a lovely cup of tea?'
Everyone shouted, 'Me, yes me!'
Herby and Mouse looked at each other,
looked at the teapot and shouted, *'Oh bother!'*

Jake Cahill (10)
St Augustine's Primary School, Camberley

GONE

In the forest animals wander around.
Birds make their nests, bees go from flower to flower.
Foxes hunt and shrews run, owls find their prey.
But then the monsters come, destroying everything.
It's all gone, nothing left.
No trees, no animals, nothing.

Jack Farnon (10)
St Augustine's Primary School, Camberley

THE DOLPHIN!

A metal shield going through the ocean
Its noise is like a mixture of potions
And all the water flows and flows
Over its sparkling eyes
Glistening silver
Squeaky voices, aqua nose
Skin really moist
The dolphin flips
The dolphin flaps
In eight seconds it did eighty claps.

Abbie Moran (9)
St Augustine's Primary School, Camberley

SOLITARY

I wait in vain,
Not looking for pain,
Only happiness and joy.

A great light shines through my jailed heart,
It rises me up to a land of love,
My heart is free of its captivity,
I'm not quite sure what I am looking at.

It looks so sweet,
Shining so bright,
But then fading,
I'm going back to the land of captivity.

Nick Lardner (10)
St Augustine's Primary School, Camberley

BOOKWORM

Owl is our class bookworm,
All quiet, timid and shy.
She likes romantic stories
And books that make you cry.

You'll never catch her swimming
Or even in New Look,
The only place you'll find her
Is curled up with a book.

She reads books all the time:
Fantasy, adventure or even hide and seek.
She reads probably two a day,
So she reads fourteen in a week.

Rachel Banks (9)
St Augustine's Primary School, Camberley

HEDGEHOG

Rustling under leaves and compost heaps
Around the garden the hedgehog creeps
With tiny eyes that see at night
One touch of the prickles would give you a fright
Its nose is small and very neat
It smells a long way
Mmm . . . what's for dinner today?

George Pilling (10)
St Augustine's Primary School, Camberley

BALD EAGLE

He is always up there,
Waiting,
Like a circling plane,
For a clearing to land
And a spider to come
Crawling along.
As he lands, he bows his bald head,
His secret weapon ready to snap
On a feast of poor, defenceless animals
Caught by the super sight of
The King of Monsters
The Bald Eagle.

John Mageean (9)
St Augustine's Primary School, Camberley

THE OCEAN'S CHILD

She lives in a world of fantasy,
A dolphin as her pet,
A bed of scale, red and blue,
Seaweed on her head.
She's a child of the ocean,
A princess of the fish,
A tail of gold, she's a jewel,
The sea urchin's only friend.
The shipwreck ruined her home,
The octopus ruined her life,
The ocean's child swims once again,
Through the ripples and the waves,
The coral and the starfish,
She swims with calm peaceful dolphin.

Natalie Garland (9)
St Augustine's Primary School, Camberley

PEACOCK

There it walks as posh as can be,
Singing, 'Look at me! Look at me!'
In her rainbow dress,
And her feathery fan,
She thinks she is the best,
Better than all the rest.

Claire Gallagher (10)
St Augustine's Primary School, Camberley

CHARGE OF THE CHEETAH BRIGADE

Half a metre, half a metre,
Half a metre onward,
Into the leopard's den,
Rode the six hundred.

Forward the cheetah brigade!
'Bomb their homes!' he said.
'Take their leader,' he said.
Onward they rampaged.

Fangs to the right of them,
Fangs to the left of them,
Fangs to the front of them,
Scratches unnumbered.

Smash - at the leopard shanks,
Smashing their nice new homes,
Taken their houses! Thanks
To the cheetah brigade
Smart six hundred.

Alex Lowe (9)
St Augustine's Primary School, Camberley

THE TIGER

You run as fast as a racing car,
Your roar echoes through the jungle,
You're so stealthy as you creep upon your prey,
Your silky fur glints in the moonlight,
You are the true hunter of Africa.

Joe Holt (10)
St Augustine's Primary School, Camberley

THE CAT

Standing on the wall
Sleek and tall
Glowing yellow eyes
Moving quietly
Creeping around.

Thomas Saunders (9)
St Augustine's Primary School, Camberley

THE FOX

It slunk silently through the narrow streets of Oxford,
My rubbish bin it knocked over as it skulked through
                          the narrow streets of Oxford,
Its gleaming eyes were like sapphires as it crept through
                          the narrow streets of Oxford,
Its tawny fur gleaming in the moonlight as it sidled through
                          the narrow streets of Oxford,
Its bottle brush tail pointing to the moon as it tiptoed through
                          the narrow streets of Oxford,
It looked at me scared and anxious and we stared at each other
                          on the narrow streets of Oxford,
Its fur on end, bearing its pearl fangs as we gazed at each other
                          on the narrow streets of Oxford,
It glared at me so scared but steady on the narrow streets of Oxford,
It scared me so I ran from the narrow streets of Oxford.

Hannah Patel (10)
St Augustine's Primary School, Camberley

THE CHINESE DRAGON

The Chinese dragon has huge fangs
a great long tail and a huge mouth.
He visits China town every year
and scares the people from far and near.
His scales are tiny and very round
he scares me when I go to China town!
His horns are curly and stick up high
and he's so big he could touch the sky!

I had a dream the other night
the dragon and I were going on a flight.
First thing I knew I was on his back,
next thing I knew we were flying back.
Over the rooftops, out of the night
into my bedroom, I shut my eyes tight!

Georgia Oakes (8)
St Catherine's School, Camberley

MY BEST FRIEND

Me and my best friend laughing
And sharing secrets never to be told
Together we have such fun
Running down the grassy hill in the summer sun
Oh! Playing together is so much fun
Her hair so shiny and long
Her blue eyes make me think of the sea
We love to be together
Her and me!

Serena Burton (8)
St Catherine's School, Camberley

HOLIDAY

H ow I love holidays when there is no work to do
O h I love holidays when you can go swimming any time
L ater on with your family you go down to the beach for a bonfire
I love holidays, they are such fun but sadly they have to end
D ance and say goodbye, back to school and homework
A way you go
Y esterday I was on holiday.

Abbey Perria (8)
St Catherine's School, Camberley

MY BOX

I will put in my box . . .
The red roses to brighten up the sky
The pink leather coat rubbing against the wet sweat.

I will put in the box . . .
A lottery ticket to make you win
The swooshing of the wind to cool me
The falling leaves to come to greet me.

I will put in my box . . .
A sparkle of a glittering star
The light moon to brighten up my box
The slithering tongue of a tiger.

I will put in my box . . .
The drops of snow
A tip of a magic finger.

My box is fashioned by pleasant things
And all my secrets have gone into a small box.

Jennifer Abel (10)
St Catherine's School, Camberley

ANGER

It sticks to you
You shake it off
But no - it will stay as long as it pleases
Watching you become furious
But it has been sent to do so
It feels bitter raw and solid
You must get rid of this anger
And feel it slowly drift away.

Victoria Beynon (10)
St Catherine's School, Camberley

THE MAGIC BOX

I will put in my box . . .
The roar of a hungry tiger
A cry of a sad whale
Photos of a holiday in the Bahamas.

I will put in my box . . .
The holler of an angry boar
The Bible of God's word
The silent prayers of the people in church.

I will put in my box . . .
The glee of a lion before he eats his prey
The broken sigh of the wind
The leg of a deadly spider.

My box is fashioned out of the finest mahogany and painted sea-blue
It has a dark blue handle with little planets moving on the lid
I will read in my box all day in a soft, comfy chair to sit in
The stories I read will be adventure and scary stories.

Rachael Curtin (9)
St Catherine's School, Camberley

ANGER

Like bullets from a gun shooting out of me
Like a volcano ready to explode
A raging hot bomb trying so hard to get out
Like a whip hitting with its fierce claws
Like a wasp's sting going through me
Like a fire burning up inside me ready to jump out
It's trapped inside me and I can't get it out
It's like a ripped piece of paper.

Roseanna Leney (9)
St Catherine's School, Camberley

JEALOUSY

It creeps round me
I feel it swirling inside me
It jabs me like a needle
Its silky body digging into me tightly
Its teeth like pins pinching me
As if it would never end.

It wraps itself round me tightly
It squirms about inside me
It knows me inside and out
It moves around and never stops.

Sarah Lapthorn (10)
St Catherine's School, Camberley

LONELINESS

Sitting on the old broken park bench
While the wind howls, tormenting her.
Once her eyes filled with pride, now lonely and sad.
Crying out, but the wind howls - no pity.
She shields her face with her arms,
Crying out for a friend, but no one heeds her.
And the wind howls on, still on.

Grace Farrell (10)
St Catherine's School, Camberley

THE MAGIC BOX

I will put in my box:
The pain of a lonely child
The smoke of a hundred cigars
The mist from a dragon's cave.

I will put in my box:
The silk cobwebs from an old house
The croak of a tired toad
The sparkle of a wand.

I will put in my box:
The tail of a mermaid
The glistening of a star
A blood red rose.

My box is fashioned from pearls to stars and thrones
Its got hidden secrets in its corners
The hinges are made of long strands of a fairy's hair
I shall lurk in my box and prick my finger upon a rose
And forever bleed.

Kesleigh Withers (10)
St Catherine's School, Camberley

STONEHENGE

The grass grabs my feet,
I hear their voices seep through the rocks
With mournful whispers,
Their hearts are filled with sorrow,
The rocks lie in grey misery,
The fire burns within the stones,
Doom lies beneath.

Claire Jones (11)
St Catherine's School, Camberley

STARRY NIGHT
(Inspired by Van Gogh's painting)

The swirling, troubled
clouds threaten.
They don't know the
trouble that's
coming.

The hills roll on
and on
until they reach
the sea.
It spins it around
like a fish
on a
line.

The stars sparkle
like a
diamond
ring,
tossed and twisted
about the
sky.

Way above it
is
rough
and
tough.
Down below
the village
settles undisturbed.

Sable Fitzgerald (11)
St Catherine's School, Camberley

STARRY NIGHT
(Inspired by Van Gogh's painting)

I gaze out
through the swirling blue sky,
down to the cypress tree
whirling and waving like seaweed.
Down to the sleeping village
and onto a lonely painter
who painted his life away.

I stare at the stars around me,
the haunting church,
the landscape
like the sea in a terrible storm
and onto a lonely painter
who painted his life away.

Emma Blott (10)
St Catherine's School, Camberley

COUNTRYSIDE WITH CYPRESSES
(Inspired by Van Gogh's painting)

Swift clouds race through the sky
Without a care
Golden corn sways from side to side
Crashes of wind thrust the trees violently
Howling like vicious dogs
But the sky stays calm and content.

I see faces in the clouds
Not happy faces
Faces with all the care in the world
Faces that screech when the wind blows
But the sky stays calm and content.

Elizabeth Anders (11)
St Catherine's School, Camberley

THE UNWANTED TOY

Jealousy builds up inside me
It's just not fair
I just sit in the corner
She looks at me with her blue eyes
I smile sweetly hoping she will play with me.

It's not fair, I am never played with
It's not fair, him and never me
I may be old and he may be new
I will probably be shifted off to a school fair tomorrow.

Hannah Martin (9)
St Catherine's School, Camberley

BEACH BATTLE

Put a shell to your ear
What can you hear?
Soldiers' cries
Swords crashing

Open your eyes
Look at the skies
The sun a canon ball
Blood-stained weapons

Pick up a shell
What can you smell?
Rotted bones
Salt from the sea.

Melanie Lovell (10)
St Catherine's School, Camberley

THE BARN OWL

His feathers are soft
His eyes are bright
He glides silently into the darkened sky
His eyes are searching for his waiting prey
He swoops down
It's gone.

Imogen Tillman (10)
St Catherine's School, Camberley

LOVE

Love is radiant, it holds out its arms
To embrace you, to wrap round you
Like a woolly blanket.
Love is comforting, love is warm
Like the south wind.
Its colours are inviting
Red like your heart and loving is in your heart.
Pink like candyfloss and as sweet
Lilac like a floating water lily.
Love brings out happy memories
It makes you feel protected
A sunny, happy feeling.

Emma Kendall (8)
St Catherine's School, Camberley

THE NIGHT APPEARS

The night appears, the black sky is starless
The damp leaves like small puddles of dew
Dogs barking on the roof, children falling asleep in their comfy beds.
As we go off hunting for food with our razor-sharp claws
And eat our prey as proud as we can
We start to fall asleep after a long day of hunting.

Farrah Amin (8)
St Catherine's School, Camberley

THE NORTH STAR

The North Star shining like a glow-worm in the sky
It is nature's guide to a lost traveller
It has felt pain and sorrow for all who have died
The North Star feels power on clear nights
It has never moved, it has seen live dinosaurs
The North Star is wise.

Esme Langford (8)
St Catherine's School, Camberley

NIGHT

Night is a peaceful time
The time when everything is dead
When the screams of the day have passed
I love it.

Night is quiet, the restful time
When the park is empty when the noise has gone
Night, what a silent, calm time.

Hannah Church (8)
St Catherine's School, Camberley

A STORM

An enormous, swirling, large object
With a freezing gust
Trying to take over the world.

When it fills with rage
Thunder and lightning
Crash to the ground
Hitting the ground and blowing up trees.
It makes you feel cold, lonely and miserable inside.

Caitlin Parker (9)
St Catherine's School, Camberley

THE RAINBOW

Look, there's a rainbow.
I'm going to see if there's treasure.
Can I go, would it be far?
I'm going to find out
Down the path, up the hills,
Look, treasure!

Niccita Singh (8)
St Catherine's School, Camberley

TEMPER

The rage, the temper,
Feeling like a volcano.
The temper is building up inside me,
I think I'm going to burst.
The lava will burn everything apart from me.
I have been annoyed,
Anger, hatred, boredom and sadness.
I may never feel the same again.
I want to be alone forever,
With only the light of a single candle,
Burning, melting, gone!

Tedi Basham (9)
St Catherine's School, Camberley

THE MAGIC BOX

I will put in my box:
Stars in the sky, an alien with four legs, a moon.
I will put in my box:
A green ladybird with black spots, a silver apple,
A golden fish, and sky with black clouds.
I will put in my box:
A little planet, some blue trees, black rain.
I will put in my box:
A coloured Earth, a blue sun.
I will put in my box:
A door into the sky, a new alphabet, new words, a new life.

Anna Bagramova (10)
St Catherine's School, Camberley

THE MAGIC BOX

I have been given this box to put in what I hold most dear.
So I shall put in . . .
The last tear of a loved one,
A memory of first steps,
The sun's rays shooting down upon the song of an angel.
I shall put in my box:
The lash of a sparrow's beak,
The last movement of a heart,
A thought of eternal life,
A gulp of water in a fatal desert.
I shall put in my box:
The smell of freshly cut grass,
The sound of the whispering wind,
Whispering in my ear,
And the taste of the morning breeze drifting by my window.
Pure is this box, so all non-believers shall never see its magic.
It lurks around corners following its heart.
I will learn in my box so I may face
The wondrous, magical world ahead in my future.

Colleen Perria (10)
St Catherine's School, Camberley

ANIMALS

Sea horses float just above the seabed
With coral and starfish all pinky-red.

Horses whinny under the starlit sky,
Not knowing there's people all sleeping by.

Cats all curled up in their snugly beds
Dreaming of hunting and hiding in sheds.

Giraffes sleeping and standing tall
Eating anything, big or small.

Hippopotamus' wallowing in lengths of mud
Sinking in water creating a flood.

Elephants trumpeting to each other
Others trumpet to their mother.

Gazelles leaping under the sun
If they see a lion they have to run.

Dogs barking through the day
Even in the sunshine of May.

Up the stairs humans creep
Just before they go to sleep.

Hollie Southey (11)
St Peter's CE (Aided) Primary School, Farnham

THE DOLPHIN

T he dolphin loves to play and play,
H e likes to play during May,
E ating fish all day long.

D olphins like to sing their favourite song,
O h their skin is grey, smooth and silky,
L ying on their backs, tummies white and milky,
P eaceful in the sea,
H aving the time of their lives while they're free,
I gnoring fishermen's nets so innocently,
N et to catch them while they should be free,
   Our hidden treasures of the sea!

Sophie Paine (10)
St Peter's CE (Aided) Primary School, Farnham

TIGERS

Tigers are so clever.
They leap and prance all over the place.
They are orange with black stripes.
They crawl in the bushes waiting to pounce.
Their fur is all hairy and fuzzy.
They climb up trees and dance around
I like *tigers!*
Because they do so many *things!*

Zachary Wynne (7)
St Peter's CE (Aided) Primary School, Farnham

THE BOUNCY BALL

The bouncy ball went down the road,
Bouncy ball hit a toad,
The bouncy ball went bouncing on
Didn't know that the toad was gone.

Josh Loftus (9)
St Peter's CE (Aided) Primary School, Farnham

RUNNING THROUGH

Running through the darkest night
Looking up on a window light
I can hear footsteps stalking through the night
So I run with all my might
Run, run, run!

Mason Redman (7)
St Peter's CE (Aided) Primary School, Farnham

ANIMALS

A   pes swing from tree to tree
N   ewts swim and dart around
I   guanas change from colour to colour
M   ice scurry along the floor into their little holes
A   nts are black, as black as the night
L   ions are big, lions are gold and they are very bold
S   nakes slither along the ground.

Ella Bennett (8)
St Peter's CE (Aided) Primary School, Farnham

PLAYING

I like playing with my PlayStation
I like playing with my Game Boy
I like playing with my ball
I like playing with my Knex
I like playing with my toys
I like playing with my big car
I like playing with my sister
I like playing with my CDs
I like playing with my colouring book
I like playing with my football stickers
I like playing with my tennis ball.

Andrew Jackson (8)
St Peter's CE (Aided) Primary School, Farnham

ROMANS

Romans were tough
Romans were strong
They were almighty
They were great conquerors
Romans were champions
Romans were great
Romans were good
Romans were brilliant
Romans were excellent
I think Romans were amazing.

Thomas Graham (7)
St Peter's CE (Aided) Primary School, Farnham

KINDNESS

K indness is helpful
I   t has love
N o it is not naughty, but
D elights in good
N ever stops
E very day it trusts and tells the truth
S o it always protects
S ays nice things as well.

Chloe Goode (7)
St Peter's CE (Aided) Primary School, Farnham

PEACE

P   eace is precious
E   veryone wants it
A   bandon wars
C   ruelty to stop
E   veryone wants peace.

Rebecca Cooles (7)
St Peter's CE (Aided) Primary School, Farnham

FOOTBALL

F ootball is really cool, you get muddy and wet.

O ur school team is really good, we pass the ball well
and score through the net.

'O h what a wonderful goal,' shout all the mums and dads.

T all players, small players, they're all really good.

B ruised after the match, got kicked in the thigh.

A ll the parents cheered us on

L osing or winning it's just for fun.

L ong waiting and we just won.

Adam Marchment (11)
St Peter's CE (Aided) Primary School, Farnham

MY CAT

My knitted, black cat, I stroke him, I cuddle him,
I talk to him in my bed with me,
My nan made him, I tell him my secrets
He sleeps in the dark cupboard,
I don't see him till the morning.

Lesley Green (7)
St Peter's CE (Aided) Primary School, Farnham

I LIKE BIRDS

I like birds when they sing to each other,
I like birds when they laugh.
I like birds that have wonderful colour.
I like different kinds of birds.
I like watching birds eat their food.
I like seeing birds fly around the garden.
I like blue tits because they are my favourite colour.
I like robins because they have red tummies,
I like kingfishers because they have wonderful colour.
I like pheasants because they have big wings.

Matthew Brown (7)
St Peter's CE (Aided) Primary School, Farnham

QUAD BIKES

Four big, black wheels,
Dull, black handlebars,
The soft leather, black seat,
The shiny, blue, plastic cover,
Once you go through the mud the wheels get really muddy,
When I am on it I feel fantastic.

Josh Injai (9)
St Peter's CE (Aided) Primary School, Farnham

IN THE . . .

In the attic . . .

Fruit bats are lurking in murky corners
An old moth-eaten briefcase of yellowing love letters
A pair of long forgotten skull-shaped earrings
With gleaming emerald eyes.
The constant dripping of a cracked water tank.

What's that groaning?
What's that moaning?
My heart is thumping!
I'm off.

Jacqueline Nevill (8)
St Peter's CE (Aided) Primary School, Farnham

FOOTBALL

It's the kick-off, now is the time
We're in red and they're in lime.
Matt kicks it to me, I kick it back
No time for a little snack.
It's very tough and very hard
We've got our defence and we've got our guard.
We're near the goal . . .
It's a goal!
Hits the goalie in the nose!
The whistle goes
What a match
Now it's time for a bath!

Matthew Bolton (8)
St Peter's CE (Aided) Primary School, Farnham

ANIMALS

Animals are fun, animals are cute
They make me smile when I'm sad
Some have legs, some can swim
I like animals, they like me
Some you can ride, some you can play with.

Animals are kind, animals can help you
Dogs, cats and horses too.
I like animals, they like me
Animals are *great!*

Emma Marriott (8)
St Peter's CE (Aided) Primary School, Farnham

MY GRANDAD IS GOD!

He can build a wall
But he can't knit at all.
He touches the mighty sky.
He makes me fly.
He loves every dog.
My grandad is God!

Charlotte Bryant (9)
The Grove Primary School